Tour the Country Roads

*Discover the Rustic Wonders
of California*

San Carlos Borromeo Mission at Carmel

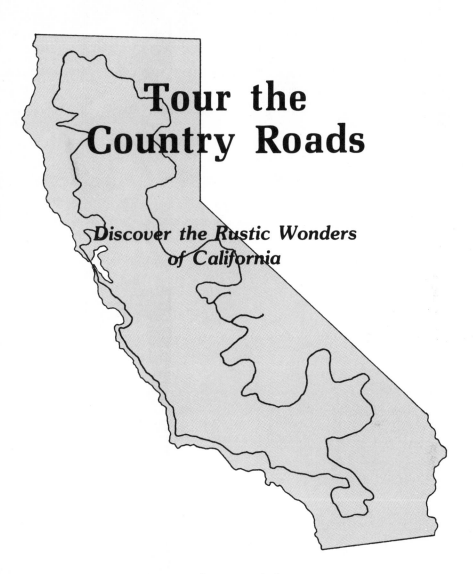

Tour the
Country Roads

*Discover the Rustic Wonders
of California*

By Arthur Reichert

Division of Book Publishers, Inc.

Fresno, CA 93728

To Betty
for her great help
in research
and for being at my side
during many months
of touring

CONTENTS

ILLUSTRATIONS

PRE-TRIP

The mention of California conveys a different picture to everyone. Your conception depends upon where you live or how much you have traveled in the state. If you've never been in California, your idea will be completely different from that of the near-native.

California is big, but the principal reason for the great variety of images of it are its many different characteristics—it seems to be made up of samples from many parts of the world. Take the tour of country roads as we did and you'll be continually reminded of other places—the Alps, the Amalfi Drive, rural England, vineyards of France, the Sahara, and New Zealand, to mention a few. This tour deals not with cities and towns but with the fascinating and beautiful regions in between. It's a discovery trip with the scene constantly changing. On it you have new and exciting experiences, see unusual and inspiring beauty, and learn about the relaxed and peaceful lives people live a few miles away from the main roads.

No attempt has been made to suggest overnight accommodations. You'll find plenty of good ones, as well as fine restaurants. One of the joys we discovered was staying in small towns. The rooms were always clean and comfortable and the people true and friendly.

Take along one of many good accommodation books. We found the AAA Tour Book useful because it is tied in with their maps of California. Wherever you are, with that book you can quickly spot a nearby place to stay.

The Auto Club divides the state into a number of areas with detailed maps showing many country roads not on larger maps. We suggest that you obtain these helpful maps.

We have divided our tour into thirteen days. As you follow it, your days will not necessarily agree in timing with ours. We suggest that you take enough time to see and feel the wonders of

California. You won't be pushed by traffic, being in the country where the pace is slower. At noon you may, as we often did, have a picnic lunch under a shady tree or beside a sparkling stream where the stirring sounds of nature emphasize the stillness. You'll soon feel the spirit, have fun, and come home with lasting memories of unforgettable experiences. Daytime is your playtime. We have mentioned few night activities because they vary with each individual. At night we enjoyed exploring the fascinating communities where we were staying. Generally, though, we turned in early, as we knew that when the sun raised the curtain on a new day, we would be anxious to see the next act and discover more of the wonders of wonderful California.

In our photos we made little attempt to show the beauties of the state. There are many fine photograph books that do that. What we did try to do was show photographs of interesting and unusual things. As you read the book, you may want to see many of these same landmarks. You'll have fun finding them and seeing them "in person." Bon voyage!

A + B

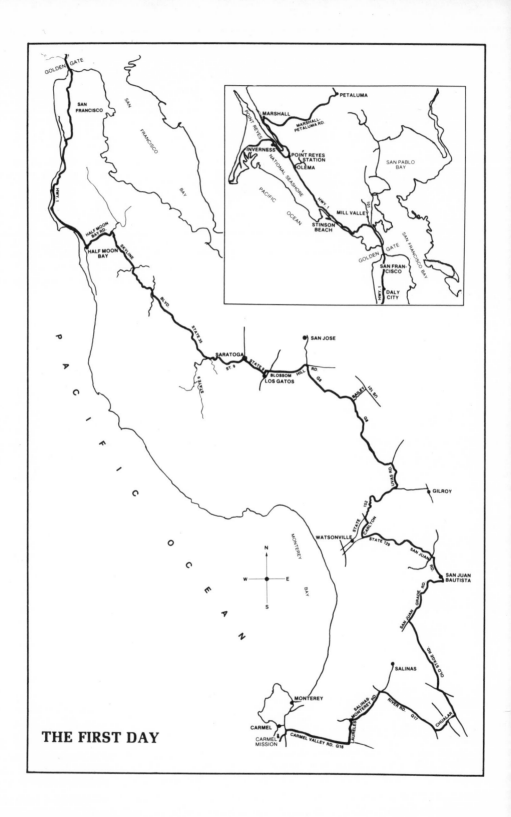

THE FIRST DAY

THE **FIRST** DAY

With great excitement and a sense of anticipation, Betty and I waved our farewells to a small group of friends as we started out on our grand tour. We were leaving from the lovely mission in Carmel, Mission San Carlos Borromeo, which was built in 1770 by Father Junipero Serra. The second of the twenty-one missions built by Father Serra, this was his favorite. He chose to make it his headquarters and is buried there.

Soon after turning onto the Carmel Valley road we began to settle down. As we passed our home Betty remarked, "Wasn't that a nice send-off they gave us?"

Still amazed that anyone had shown up so early to see us off, I replied, "Yeah, you'd think we were going on a grand tour around the world instead of just California."

"But this is going to be so different," Betty said enthusiastically. "Just think! No freeways—all country roads!"

Already thinking about the oil, battery, water and tires, I uttered, "Uh, huh."

She continued, "You'll be taking hundreds of wonderful photographs...Did you bring your camera?"

At Mid-Valley we passed an old barn which prompted Betty to ask, "Why don't they tear down that ramshackle old barn?"

"That old barn," I told her, "is the most painted barn on the Monterey Peninsula."

In disbelief she said, "Looks like it's *never* been painted."

As I stopped the car I explained, "It has been painted again and again by artists. If it is such a good subject for a painting, maybe it should be our first picture!"

Eleven miles from the mission we turned north on Los Laureles Grade Road, leaving pleasant, and as yet unspoiled, Carmel Valley to go over the mountain. As we reached the top, Betty exclaimed, "Look, you can see Salinas! It's so quiet and beautiful up here."

Old barn in Carmel Valley. A favorite of artists.

Also enjoying the view, I said, "That's why this was one of the first roads in California to be designated a scenic highway."

"Which road was number one?"

"Number One," I answered.

"That's what I asked."

"That's what I answered." I tried to clarify things. "California State Route Number One was designated first."

We turned right on the Monterey-Salinas Road and then in a few miles took the Reservation Road to the little town of Chualar. This whole area, which is part of the prosperous Salinas Valley made famous by the writings of John Steinbeck, is beautiful and fertile farm land. From this valley artichokes, lettuce and many other fine vegetables are shipped throughout the country.

About a mile beyond Chualar we headed north on the Old Stage Road. I remarked that it was the original road from Salinas to San Juan Bautista when stagecoaches traveled this area. Now people take Highway 101. Betty responded happily, "I like this better."

We continued through rolling ranch country. Cattle were grazing. Large fields of grain surrounded us. Clumps of bushy trees dotted the countryside. The only evidence of man was an occasional ranch complex of house, barns and other out-buildings nestled in the distance.

Betty remarked about the strange appearance of the roadbed. "I think it's beautiful!" I said enthusiastically. "It's concrete laid like a sidewalk probably fifty to sixty years ago. And look—it's still in good shape."

As we neared San Juan Bautista the countryside began to change with the appearance of many little farms and small houses. In San Juan Bautista we stopped at the enchanting old square where the stages once stopped.

This great square, which in the early days was probably dirt, is now soft green grass surrounded by the mission (built in 1797), a hotel, livery stables, a boarding and rooming house, saloon and other old buildings. All have been preserved or lovingly restored. The large livery stable houses original coaches, buggies and surreys with fringe on top. You could easily spend all day happily browsing around this unique place, dreaming of living in the past.

The town itself, established in 1869, is preserved in a fascinating way, with hardly a touch of today. On our way through the village I snapped the delightful "City Library."

3

Mission at San Juan Bautista, founded in 1797.

San Juan Bautista City Library.

Leaving San Juan Bautista we traveled through a flat valley of small farms, but as soon as we had crossed Freeway 101 we immediately found ourselves in hilly, rolling, grazing country—quite scenic and quiet.

Near Watsonville are extensive orchards, mostly apple, for which Watsonville is noted. We missed Watsonville by turning onto Carlton Road, a short cut to State 152. This road over Hecker Pass climbs and winds through stately evergreens.

In Uvas Valley we discovered many small wineries. The valley was originally settled by Italians whose descendants have prospered by continuing the vineyards, wineries, and traditions. We found it fun to winery-hop, tasting the various vintages of many fine wines. It's a beautiful valley—in fact, the whole trip from San Juan Bautista to the outskirts of San Jose is stimulating.

Reaching State 9 we were again on a Scenic Highway, through Saratoga and Los Gatos. Betty was moved by these two quiet and enchanting towns and remarked, "Wouldn't Saratoga be an exciting place to live—or retire to?"

It is understandable why so many people come here to live. We decided that sometime we, too, should like to have a "charming little cottage" here.

We reached Skyline Boulevard, another Scenic Highway, and traveled along a high sunny ridge of mountains looking down to inviting valleys on both sides. It's an inspiring trip and the road is certainly deserving of the designation of Scenic Highway.

Twenty-six miles farther this all-too-short ridge trip ended as we turned toward Half Moon Bay, on an enjoyable road between mountains.

As we neared the ocean we passed ranches, grazing land, large greenhouses, and tremendous fields of flowers planted for seed. Around Half Moon Bay, a town of about 5,100 people, are grown many varieties of vegetables. The area is famous nationwide for pumpkins.

At the ocean we followed the beautifully rugged shore, a drive climaxed by a run over the majestic Golden Gate Bridge.

Highway One led us along the still craggy shore by popular Stinson Beach and through luxurious Muir Woods. The densely wooded area is almost like a jungle. After a winding, hilly, exciting, mountain-hugging ride above the ocean, we came down to ocean level at Point Reyes Station.

Crossing an old bridge, we soon reached the quiet and peaceful village of Inverness, our destination for Day Number One. We enjoyed an excellent dinner in one of two well-known Czech restaurants—and so to bed in a comfortable boatel on the quiet shore of Tomales Bay.

Half Moon Bay claims to be the Pumpkin Center of the world.

THE SECOND DAY

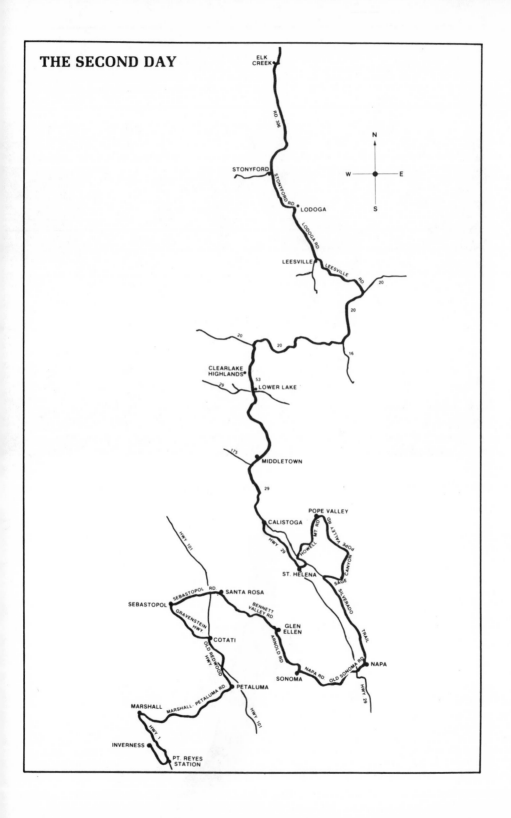

THE **SECOND** DAY

In the brisk early morning air we explored the long, narrow, unspoiled peninsula known as Tomales Bay State Park. It was a gratifying experience. We returned to Inverness where Betty mailed a letter at the little Post Office and I took a picture of a unique library which must be the smallest public library in the world. Then, rejoining State Route 1, we headed north along beautiful Tomales Bay.

To enjoy it fully, we made the drive slowly. We saw the name Drake often; Sir Francis Drake is supposed to have landed near here in about 1577. At the start of the drive the Bay was narrow and the beach sandy, but as we drove on it widened somewhat and became rocky and we saw more boats, both fishing and pleasure.

Betty, looking at the still bay where a slight haze was rising from the water, suddenly exclaimed, "We forgot! We forgot to have oysters last night. Tomales Bay is famous for delicious oysters. Look at all those oyster traps."

I corrected her. "Oyster beds."

"Same thing."

"Not to oysters; they prefer beds."

We were intrigued by the unusual shape of a small dingy which seemed worth a picture. In talking to an old-timer who was standing nearby, we learned that he had built the foreign-looking dingy and also the large boat to which it was moored. He said he had been working on the large boat for thirty years and when it is finished he expects to take a long trip, maybe around the world. He seemed like a happy old man. As we left, we wished him good sailing.

Beyond the Marshall Post Office we turned onto Petaluma Road. Just up the hill is a curious old Russian Church overlooking the Bay. An interesting and modern A-frame structure in front of the church supports a bell with the inscription, "Peace Bell—St. Helen's Mission, 1974." The sleek new structure in contrast to the old mission

9

THE SECOND DAY

This may be the smallest public library in the U.S.

Dinghy of unique design along East Shore Road of Tomales Bay.

Peace Bell at old Russian mission outside Marshall.

certainly symbolizes the changes that have taken place since the mission was founded more than 100 years ago by the Russians.

Petaluma Road starts out winding and rocky, surrounded by low, wild vegetation—quite beautiful. The scene soon changes into a real old-time rural area with large farm houses, lazy dairy cows in pleasant pastures, old rail fences—but still rocky. We were reminded of many farm areas of Europe.

We discovered Petaluma to be a small city which has carefully preserved its fine old buildings and early western charm. It was founded in 1851. Despite obvious growth it is still an engaging country town, noted as the center for many poultry farms. The people are friendly and unhurried.

We drove north on Petaluma Boulevard on our way to Sebastopol, which was probably named after the Russian city or bay of the same name. The sign outside of town says, "Founded in 1853"— so it figures, for at that time many Russians lived in this area.

THE SECOND DAY

State 12 took us to Santa Rosa, another old city of 70,000 in the fertile Sonoma Valley. Founded in 1833, it is noted for various fruits. Luther Burbank had his home and gardens here, and this is where he did much of his work, developing hundreds of varieties of flowers, vegetables, and fruits, including prunes.

Betty surprised me: "Too bad Mr. Burbank died so soon."

Wondering, I asked why. "He became a very old and great man and achieved hundreds of successes in creating many new foods we enjoy today."

"Yes—but prunes still have wrinkles."

On the Bennett Valley Road toward Sonoma we traveled through a quiet, blissful, distinctly rural valley with mountains on all sides.

At Kenwood we took Warm Springs Road, continuing in the same beautiful Bennett Valley. We stopped to examine an old stone fence that typifies the area. Roads there are tunnels through overhanging trees with sunlight sprinkling through. Ivy grows on houses and trees. There are few farm houses and little traffic. An old A-frame bridge is haloed by lush, bushy trees. The whole area reminded us of England.

Glen Ellen is a quaint, sleepy town with a cute little post office. The old Chavet Hotel, built seventy years ago, has stained glass windows and charming architecture. There are lots of antiques in Glen Ellen. Even though Jack London was born in San Francisco and has a square named for him in Oakland, it is evident he "once slept here." His name is on food and wine shops, a book store, a gallery—the town is a haven for Jack London memorabilia. Betty said she bet Glen Ellen attracts a lot of tourists, to which I quipped, "Sort of a 'call of the wild.'"

Farther on, in the center of the old town of Sonoma, is a large tree-shaded park and square. On the southeast corner of the square stands the refreshingly simple and beautiful San Francisco de Solano Mission, built in 1823. The first hotel operated north of San Francisco (built in the early 1840s) and many other historical landmarks attract today's traveler.

I mentioned, "Here's where it all started."

"The wine business?" asked Betty.

"No, the Republic of California. General Fremont founded it 'way back in 1846."

"That was before the Gold Rush. Why did they ever unfound the Republic?"

We saw many old stone fences like this one in Bennett Valley.

Typical farm house between Marshall and Petaluma.

San Francisco de Solano Mission at Sonoma, founded in 1823.

Old wagon resting in the shade in the village of Pope Valley.

"The Gold Rush rapidly brought tremendous changes in California and soon the people here wanted to join the U.S. There was quite a battle, but we became a state, anyway."

Not giving up, Betty replied, "Too bad. Wish we were still a Republic. Out here we're different from all those people in the East. Why should they run us?" After hesitation and some thought, she continued, "And maybe then we could keep them from coming out here in droves. In a few years beautiful California will be gone. Let's start a Bear Flag march on Washington to get our freedom back."

At Napa, which was settled in 1840 and is now the gateway to California's great wine country, we took the famous Silverado Trail north through the sunny, lush, grape-growing Napa Valley. Many of the big wineries celebrated for their fine wines are located there.

Lake Hennessey, a large man-made reservoir in the Lake Hennessey Recreational Area, like so many artificial lakes in California, looks natural and beautifully inviting.

15

THE SECOND DAY

We proceeded toward the village of Pope Valley through an enchanting and seemingly uninhabited valley. A sparkling stream accompanied us.

We stopped at the Pope Valley Post Office. Reading the sign above the door, Betty mentioned that the population of the town is 94,567.

Skeptical, I said, "Oh, there can't be more than ninety-four people in this little village."

She pointed to the sign. "Says so right there."

I smiled. "At least they have a big zip code number."

Pope Valley is a delightful village. An old blacksmith shop still stands there. The sign outside says, "Henry Haus Blacksmith and Wagonmaker." Beside the shop is a fascinating old wagon which Henry Haus probably built long ago, and the original forge is still there.

Leaving Pope Valley, we began climbing and winding. It is an excitingly beautiful trip over the mountain from Pope Valley back to Napa Valley, with dense woods near the top.

As we entered Angwin, a little college town nestled in the foothills, we found Pacific Union College, with its spectacularly modern buildings. We especially admired the elegant bell tower and the huge auditorium topped by a big dome.

Soon we crossed the Silverado Trail and continued on to St. Helena where many well-known wineries are located. Because of its lovely setting and reputation for fine wine, we joined ten others for a tour through the Beringer Winery. We were fortunate to be on a tour conducted by a highly knowledgeable wine expert. The Beringer Winery is carved out of the side of a stone mountain, with row after row of huge wine casks stored in this cool cave. The natural temperature remains ideal and unvaried throughout the year. Our tour guide explained in detail the delicate process of making wine, and we left feeling happy and well informed.

After a brief stop at Calistoga, a health resort with nearby hot mineral springs and geysers, we proceeded to State 20. The first part is an unspoiled wildnerness—winding and hilly. This soon changes and the drive follows a cheerful stream for many miles, then goes through a pleasant broad valley. Our planned route was to leave State 20 nine miles west of Williams and head for Lodoga, Stonyford and Elk Creek, but because of a scarcity of suitable lodging in that area, we skipped over to Willows for the night.

Bandstand at St. Helena.

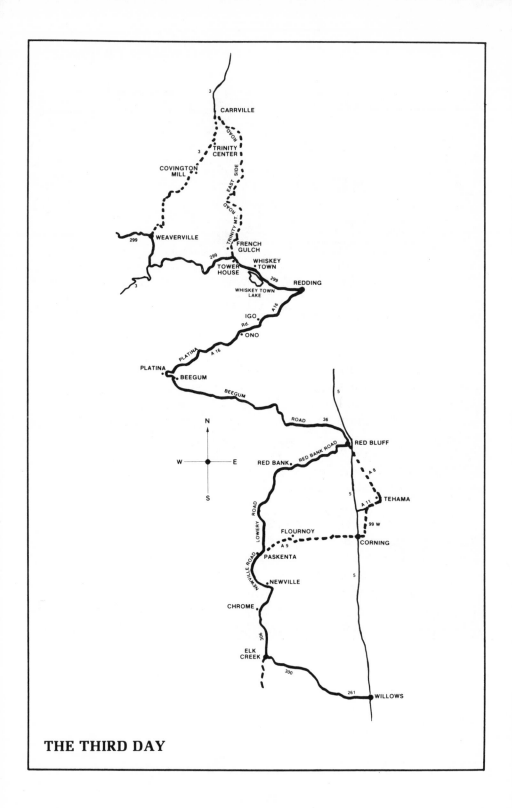

THE THIRD DAY

THE **THIRD** DAY

On the road from Willows to Elk Creek (State 162), we traveled across a wide plain with low mountains in the distance. Fertile farm land with tremendous fields of gently flowing grain surrounded us.

Betty remarked about the stillness and absence of traffic, the beauty of wide open country space, the fresh clean air, the relaxed feeling of not being pushed. "What an exhilarating feeling, to start a new day like this," she said.

"Such a cool, crisp morning . . . there's nothing better than a good ol' country road in the morning to make you feel alive and eager to see what the new day brings . . . "

She interrupted me with, "Let's get a little place in the country somewhere."

I was apprehensive. "Be farmers? What do we know about farming? What would we raise? Besides, it's hard work . . . "

"Bees!" Betty broke in excitedly.

"In the car?" I was alarmed.

"No, silly. Look over there at all those beehives. See, we could have a honey farm. The bees do all the work. They've had years of experience. You don't have to plant them. They raise their own workers and send them out into the fields to harvest. Then they bring in the crop and store it in those little barns."

"Sounds sweet."

Out of Elk Creek, a small, slow-moving rural village, we followed the gently flowing Elk Creek and headed north toward Paskenta. As we proceeded we saw several more large groups of beehives. Maybe there really are bee farms.

We stopped at an old cemetery that attracted our attention. Everything there is stark white and gray. No grass—the ground is gray gravel of various sizes. At the back of the cemetery are a water tower, windmill and a large tree—no other foliage anywhere on the grounds. Some of the markers are wood with inscriptions long since

19

No grass in this old cemetery near Elk Creek, but it does have a windmill and water tank.

faded. The tallest stone monument is dated 1892, the one next to it 1876. Interestingly, there are several new stones with dates in the 1800s, indicating that the original markers had been weathered away and recently replaced. I mentioned that there must be descendants nearby who come to check things and have restored or replaced old monuments. "What gets me is why they don't put in some grass and plant a few bushes—tidy up the place."

Giving one last look, Betty said, "Guess they want to keep it unspoiled."

A little farther on, the village of Chrome presented two houses with barns, an unusual water tower with a curious metal base, and more beehives. We drove through Newville but missed it. Maybe it isn't as big as Chrome.

Entering Paskenta, we found the first building to be the Lazy Z

Well-supported old water tank at Chrome.

Bar Saloon. Paskenta is a seemingly sleepy village on the Thames Creek. As we left we passed "The Club - Cocktails - Cafe." A sign on its door reads, "Shoes and Shirts Mandatory — No Minors Allowed."

Betty's comment: "Must be a stuffy place."

We proceeded toward Red Bank through rolling country, the road bordered by great fields of grain and pasture, with some cows and a few farm houses—probably large ranches. Everything was brown—hardly a tree or shrub anywhere. Near one old ranch house were beehives, but the house was deserted. We saw many more abandoned farm houses as we drove along. Either past homesteaders had given up or the land is now in the hands of large operators. Finally we came to a big occupied farm house with a

One farmer near Red Bank has his own idea about mailboxes.

We saw many colonies of bees like this one.

number of barns, all newly painted in bright red. The house was stark yellow. Across the road from the house was a cattle loader vividly painted in the same yellow.

"Paint a cattle loader! They must have had some yellow paint left over," I suggested.

As we crossed clear-running Elder Creek we came to a long row of mail boxes, although only one house was in view in the far distance. One of the mail boxes, designed like an old barn, showed imagination.

We came to another group of beehives. Having seen so many, we finally decided to get a picture.

From Paskenta to Red Bank the way is lonely. We saw only one car and two people. The area is not particularly inviting and the gravel road is less comfortable than some might like. (Note: To avoid this road, take A-9 out of Paskenta to Corning, then A-11 and A-8 to Red Bluff.) Out of Red Bluff we took Beegum Road toward Platina.

Betty looked at the map. "We're headed for Beegum on the Beegum Road."

"Right," I replied, uninterested.

She went on, "Also Platina on the Platina River. Then on to Ono and Igo. We cross Grizzly Creek and Piddlers Creek..."

Now interested, I pulled up and quickly took the map. "Let me see that—that's Fiddlers Creek!"

"Well, anyway, over there is Lazyman Butte, then Peanut Mountain and beyond that Hay Fork Summit. We are going to Whiskeytown near Brandy Creek. We just miss Knob Peak near Cow Gulch. What county are we in?"

Again losing interest, I answered, "Tehama."

"See, I told you."

"You haven't told me anything yet. What's all this leading to?" Betty persisted. "He didn't make much sense."

"Who didn't?"

"The fellow who named the places around here. He had no imagination. Why couldn't he have used simple, logical names, like Junipero Serra, San Luis Obispo, San Juan Bautista..."

I broke in. "Never mind—you must be getting homesick."

Between Red Bluff and Beegum is cheerful farm and timber country. Beegum turned out to be a tiny old village serving the farmers of the area. About a mile farther we joined Platina Road

23

and traveled through Ono and Igo, two small villages on our way toward Redding, the county seat of Shasta County. On the Sacramento River, Redding, founded in 1873, has become a tourist center for this beautiful and exciting mountainous region called the Whiskeytown Shasta-Trinity National Recreation Area.

We were both enthralled with the area. I explained that this whole region is one big playground, an area where progress has come but not spoiled the natural setting.

Betty said, "I don't see any progress or any changes. It all looks like lovely wilderness to me. Just look at this nice blue Whiskeytown Lake that we are traveling beside..."

"That's what I mean. That's a dammed lake..."

Betty was shocked. "Polluted?"

"No, no, that beautiful lake is a modern reservoir created by the Whiskeytown Dam. There's also Shasta Lake with its Shasta Dam and Trinity Lake with its Trinity Dam. Look on the map. Those three lakes provide flood control, tremendous amounts of electric power and irrigation. That's great progress by man that even improves upon nature—without spoiling nature."

Betty was intrigued with the name Whiskeytown and was eager to see the town. We found it to be a Post Office, general store, and gas station, all in one building, and that is the only building in the "great and exciting" Whiskeytown.

Betty said hopefully, "Well, on to French Gulch... *that* ought to be something."

We had planned to take Trinity Mountain Road to French Gulch and on to the Trinity-Lewiston area with its long Clair Eagle Lake. Trinity Mountain Road from French Gulch on around the lake to Weaverville is said to be beautiful and spectacular. As we approached it, Betty said with excitement, "There's the road to French Gulch!"

"We aren't taking it."

"Not going to chic French Gulch?"

"Look at the time and look at the map. We can't be sure there's a place to stay on the loop to Weaverville and we'd never make Weaverville by nightfall. I suggest we go directly to Weaverville."

Betty was plainly disappointed. "I so wanted to see French Gulch."

"We'll see it next time," I promised.

The road from Redding to Weaverville was as delightful as

One of America's first condominiums, in Weaverville.

always. The trees and foliage are lush and green. The gently winding road keeps rising until it reaches 4,543 feet. After a gratifying and most beautiful trip we entered Weaverville, a small enchanting town founded in 1850. We cruised around a bit, finding the village and its old buildings extremely fascinating. Court Street has many old, well-maintained and lovely homes. One in particular, the Regan house, a sort of miniature of a fine old mansion, is famous for its elegant architecture. On the main street is an old stone building with windows that are merely openings in the thick stone walls. The window coverings are iron plates that swing open on great iron hinges, with much creaking. The building is now a tavern.

In the middle of town across from each other are two charming and unusual old buildings with outside spiral staircases which lead from the street to second floor balconies. A plaque on one of the buildings told us that they were early-day condominiums, built about 1855. The lower floor was owned and lived in by one party, the upper floor by another. Through the years the floors have changed hands, though the lower floor of the condominium on the south side of the street has always been a grocery store. These two attractive buildings, which had been freshly painted white, are typical of the remarkable old architecture that we found throughout Weaverville.

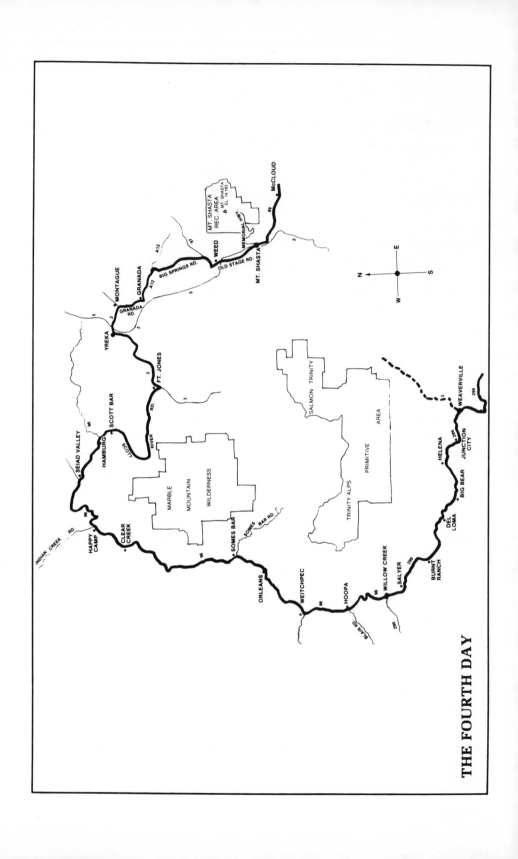

THE FOURTH DAY

THE **FOURTH** DAY

The next morning we were awakened by the crow of a nearby rooster, breaking the early-morning quiet.

"What's that?" asked Betty.

"A rooster crowing—and before you ask why, he's staking out his claim on all the chickens within hearing of his crow," I told her.

"They all come running, eh?"

"No, not really. Actually they don't seem to pay much attention to him."

"Liberated, I s'pose."

We continued to explore Weaverville. The old Chinese Joss House has been there since the founding of the town. Part of the outside of the building has been attractively restored. The other weather-worn part has been preserved as it has always been. Inside everything remains seemingly untouched. There are a few benches but it appears that, as in China, these earlier people sat on the floor. The stove is particularly interesting. Through a unique arrangement the heat and smoke, from a six-foot firebed underneath, travel through a combination of metal tunnels and a chimney. The heat is cleverly extracted by the tunnels to heat the room while the cooled smoke flows out through the chimney. This exotic Joss House is reported to be the oldest Chinese temple in California. We were disappointed not to be able to get a photograph because of the many surrounding trees.

We left Weaverville, headed toward Willow Creek and were soon in magnificent country. A mile beyond Oregon Mountain Pass (2,902 feet) we came to the LaGrange Mine where in the old gold days 100,000 yards of gravel-land was removed to recover $3,500,000 worth of gold. "That's a lot of gold," Betty pondered.

"I suppose for one mine—and that's probably at the old price of $35 per ounce. Figure what it would be worth at say $175 an ounce," I added.

27

THE FOURTH DAY

"This seems an unlikely place. Where *do* they find gold?"

Well, actually, gold is widely distributed in many lands and large amounts are present in the sea."

"I've heard stories of old prospectors dying in the desert, but I never heard of one drowning in the deep."

"Someday you might, but right now with current methods the cost of recovering gold from the sea generally exceeds the value of the gold. Old-timers could search for gold alone. For undersea recovery you need a big operation with a lot of capital."

"Maybe those oil fellows should keep an eye open for gold when they're drilling."

The trip from Weaverville to Willow Creek was spectacular. At Junction City, which is really a village with only a few buildings, a general store, and a tavern, we crossed Canyon Creek, which flows into Trinity River. The Trinity, twenty to forty feet wide, runs through exquisite, densely-wooded country with rugged mountains on both sides.

We stopped often to admire the great beauty, still unspoiled, that nature so generously spread along the valley of the Trinity. Soon after we entered Six Rivers National Forest we were surprised to find a small museum in that vast wilderness. An old ore car stands in front and inside are all sorts of relics from the area. Rocks, bottles, machinery and many other things are well arranged and clean. The windows have cross-hatched iron grilling so even if the glass panes were broken you couldn't get in. The owner's little cottage is in the rear.

Willow Creek is a quiet, pleasant village of 1,050 people. Before heading north toward Somes Bar we stopped for gas. The station is modern except for an old-timer sitting in a chair leaning back against the wall, content to watch the little-changing scene. I asked him about the road to Somes Bar.

"Well, it ain't one of them freeways, but it sure is pretty," he replied. He seemed puzzled when I told him that was just what we were looking for.

We followed the canyon of the Trinity, the road high on the side of the mountain. The scene is unbelievably beautiful. The mountains are close on both sides, with lovely green trees above and below. As we looked down, the wide sunlit river sparkled at us. With practically no traffic we had a comfortable relaxed feeling and drove slowly to make it last.

Deep in the forest west of Weaverville we found this little museum.

At Orleans we found a small hotel and quite a few homes and other buildings spread out along the main street. The village gives the appearance of being a bit unkempt.

Betty said, "It's a gyp, naming a place like this after Old Orleans."

"You mean New Orleans."

"Yes, old New Orleans."

A few blocks farther on I was amused at the name Ishi Pishi Road. Betty observed that it sounded like a better name for the town than Orleans.

As we followed the Klamath River on our way to Happy Camp we came to a widening of the canyon where Irving Creek joins the Klamath River. Far below we could see the Blue Herron Ranch. It is a beautiful picture—a heavenly farm area closed in on all sides by majestic mountains, two clear, sparkling streams meandering their ways around this island paradise.

Betty was thrilled with the view. "I hope no developer finds that lovely hideaway."

I was excited, too. "With a place like that I could enjoy farming. Just think. We could forget all activities in Washington, Israel, Europe, Peking, Moscow, Africa... All our problems would fade away."

Betty brought us back to reality by wondering where the nearest shopping center is.

The river and the mountains and the ever-changing varieties of trees continued as the road took us through Happy Camp and Seiad Valley.

At Hamburg we went south on the Scott River Road toward Fort Jones. The fast-flowing Scott River is enchanting. The valley has a surprisingly large variety of trees and bushes, quite different from the Klamath canyon.

Three miles ahead, directly across from a typical old school where children were playing in recess, is a monument to John Scott, who first discovered gold in this area in 1850.

As we traveled along Scott River, immense, smooth boulders reminded us of Yosemite. Outside of Fort Jones is a fairly flat, wide valley with low mountains in the distance. We were back in farm country, but soon started a steady climb to Forest Mountain pass (4,159 feet) and then began the descent to Yreka. To make an enjoyable road even more beautiful, we soon had our first glimpse of snow-topped, majestic Mt. Shasta.

"What's that mountain?" asked Betty.

"Must be Mt. Shasta—it's got a white top. We're approaching it from the north—so we'll go around it and to the east. It should be our companion for a long time. Tonight we'll sleep by its side."

"What a lovely thought."

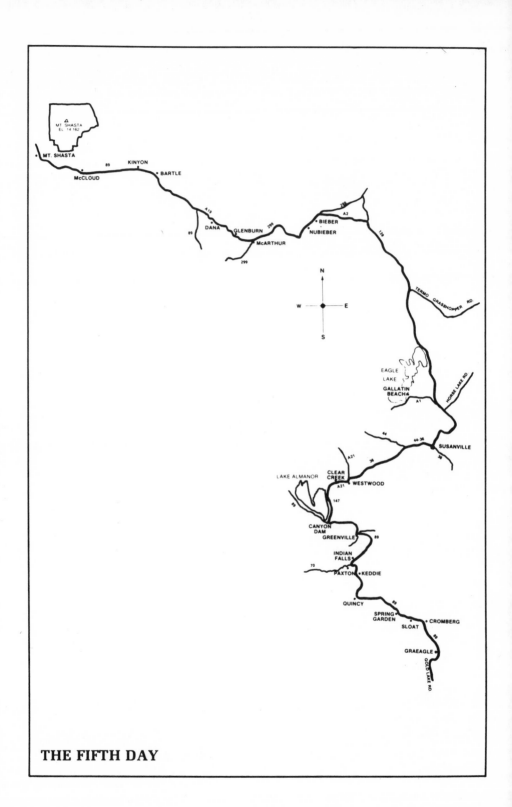

THE FIFTH DAY

THE **FIFTH** DAY

Mt. Shasta country is beautiful, with vast areas of wilderness, lakes, and recreation lands. Here thousands enjoy fishing, hunting, skiing, and boating. Just to travel through casually as we did gave us a new appreciation of how wonderful the "wonders of nature" can be.

Leaving the little resort town of Mt. Shasta we became even more conscious of the exquisiteness of the area. The stately fir and pines leaned over to whisper to us as we passed. We saw no houses or people, just queenly Mt. Shasta nearby, seeming to guard the precious peace of her mighty domain.

We heard a loud shot. "What's that?" cried Betty.

"A hunter. I believe this is the first day of the hunting season."

"How could he? He just killed our musement."

"*Musement*? You mean amusement?"

"No, musement. He destroyed our wonderment, our amazement...we were having beautiful daydreams conjured up by this inspiring beauty and he..."

I interrupted, "I'll bet the hunting is great around here."

We climbed slowly. At Dead Horse Summit the elevation is 4,535 feet. Soon we were out of the woods and back to civilization. A sign said to watch out for livestock, and sure enough, almost immediately a group of twenty-five to thirty cows came leisurely toward us. We slowed down. After eyeing us carefully they parted and let us pass.

A short distance farther on we were in the midst of a wide level valley with mountains on both sides—and good ol' Shasta still in the distance. This is prosperous farm country. I took a picture of an old windmill—really old—its blades battered, shingle roof all weatherbeaten. To complete the image, it was standing beside a drooping, half-dead tree. The house alongside also had seen better days.

Abandoned windmill near Glenburn.

Lonesome house near Glenburn. Mt. Shasta is in the distance.

A little farther along we came to an abandoned and lonesome three-story farmhouse in the middle of a huge field. In the distance Mt. Shasta still stood guard. A minute later we were in Glenburn, which consists of an inviting, old white church, a typical country general store, and a tiny post office. The whole area is delightfully rural and quiet with only a few small houses and barns scattered about.

At McArthur we started climbing toward Bieber and soon reached Big Valley Summit (4,603 feet), with a fine view of the broad plains in the distance. We began the descent into Big Valley. This is high country with the valley plains at levels around 3,000 feet.

In Grasshopper Valley, still high up, we saw serene Eagle Lake in the distance. Our road took us along its shore for quite a few miles.

Church in Glenburn. There is also a general store.

Several large old buildings are being restored in Westwood.

Betty remarked, "Coot Lake."

"It's a big lake," I answered, "but I wouldn't call it cute."

"I didn't say cute. Look at all those coots. Should have named it Coot Lake instead of Eagle. And look on the map—it's shaped like an unborn babe. Map namers just have no imagination."

Slowing up, I suggested, "Here's a nice spot. Let's have lunch on 'Embryo' Lake."

Out of Susanville we gradually climbed until we reached Fredonyer Pass (5,748 feet), then descended into Westwood, which proved to be unique and curious. One old section is being restored. Several of the buildings are unusually large for such a small town.

Lake Almanor seemed to be a happy resort with many cottages and a number of motels and lodges nestled along the shore. The lake looked so inviting that we decided to stay for the night but found that it was a busy weekend and a popular place. There were no rooms available.

Our trip south that afternoon took us through the clean, charming village of Greenville. We followed Indian Creek, Spanish Creek and Greenborn Creek. That whole area is incredibly refreshing. In the gushing streams white water rushes around tremendous boulders.

Beyond Quincy we began to follow the famous, fabulous Feather River, and soon reached Graeagle, where we stayed for several days of golf, relaxing and exploring the charming area. Graeagle is a quiet, cheerful village with a unique charm. Years ago it was a sawmill town. Today the company homes are colorfully painted red with white trim and house quaint little shops, stores and offices.

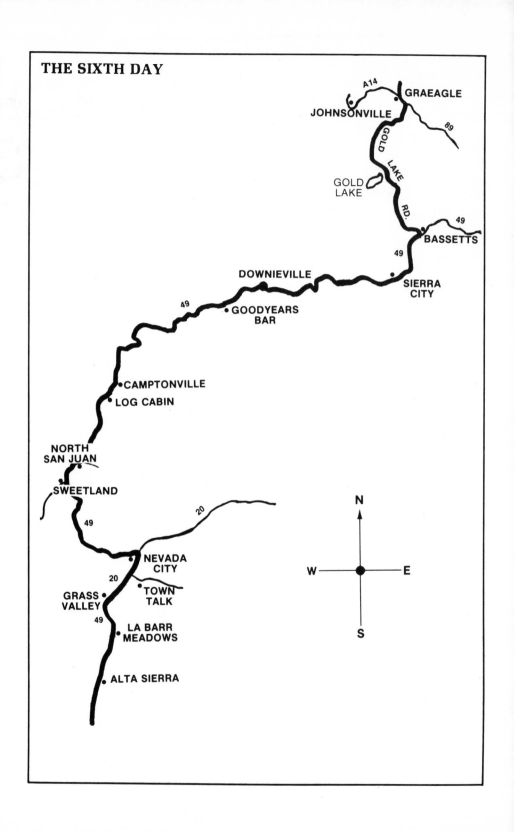

THE SIXTH DAY

JOHNSONVILLE
A14
GRAEAGLE
89
GOLD LAKE RD.
GOLD LAKE
49
BASSETTS
49
SIERRA CITY
DOWNIEVILLE
49
GOODYEARS BAR
CAMPTONVILLE
LOG CABIN
NORTH SAN JUAN
SWEETLAND
49
20
NEVADA CITY
20
TOWN TALK
GRASS VALLEY
49
LA BARR MEADOWS
ALTA SIERRA

N
W   E
S

THE **SIXTH** DAY

After a pleasant weekend in the Graeagle area we continued south on Gold Lake Road. The region is densely wooded, rugged, and rocky. Luxurious wilderness surrounded us on all sides as we made the climb. We were delighted with Gold Lake, a quiet, deep blue jewel of a lake set in the mountains at an elevation of 6,409 feet (higher than Tahoe). The trip between Graeagle and State 49 reminded us again of the many magnificent, unspoiled areas of California that can only be reached by little traveled "side" roads.

As we began our journey on Scenic Highway 49, we stopped to read a roadside marker: "Site of the Howard Ranch and Inn 1865. The log cabin inn was rebuilt and renamed Bassett House by Marion Jacobs Bassett in 1871. The stopover was used by stage and freight teams between Truckee, Sierraville, Gold Lake and Downieville until 1906. No wayfarer ever went away hungry from Bassett House." This area with its one store is now called Bassett's Station.

A little farther on we entered Sierra City, a small, quaint old village with buildings and homes closely hugging the road. The old Ore House is still there and also a Mountain Madness restaurant. Sierra Butte Inn surely came out of the 1850s. As we left the town we spotted a fascinating well near an old white house. The bottom of the well-house is weathered stone and the roof is heavy copper, aged to a warm old green.

Along State 49 the scenery continued to be excitingly beautiful, densely wooded with many different species of trees scattered among the stately evergreens.

As we entered Downieville we were greeted by two charming old houses. The upstairs porch of one was almost completely covered with luxurious vines. The little house next door is occupied by the local newspaper, called the *Mountain Messenger*, established in 1853.

The roof of this well just outside of Sierra City is well-weathered copper.

Downieville has many delightful old buildings.

As the sign says, "A Way of Life."

Near the center of town a curious iron tower supports Downieville's fire bell. Caged within the tower is a living evergreen tree, decorated with "Christmas tree lights," which cheers the village throughout the year. Downieville is enchanting—it gives you the warm feeling that it has seen little change since the early gold rush days.

THE SIXTH DAY

Along the Yuba River we traveled through miles and miles of exquisite, unspoiled wilderness, discovering yet another of the many beauty-areas of California. At one point the boulders are tremendous. With a clear view down the rapidly flowing stream, we stopped to appreciate the grandeur.

Betty said, "It's Yosemite all over again."

I was excited. "I could take dozens of great photos here but they still couldn't tell the story. It's the bigness of the area that a photograph can't catch. Look at those giant rounded boulders, the big mountains all around, the great trees ..."

"Only we are small," Betty observed.

"You said it. And there are too many small people in the world. If nature can do such big and beautiful things, why can't people?"

"They should sit on this rock and be inspired."

We soon came to Nevada City, which was laid out in 1849. We were reminded of its roaring past—all the gold that came from here—its uncontrolled saloon days. A few landmarks remain, but Nevada City, now in the midst of big orchards and a widespread recreation area, sadly (or maybe fortunately), "ain't what it used to be."

After exploring Nevada City we went on to Alta Sierra, where we knew of a quiet motel on a hilly little golf course that we liked.

Bell tower on the square in Downieville.
A permanent Christmas tree grows inside.

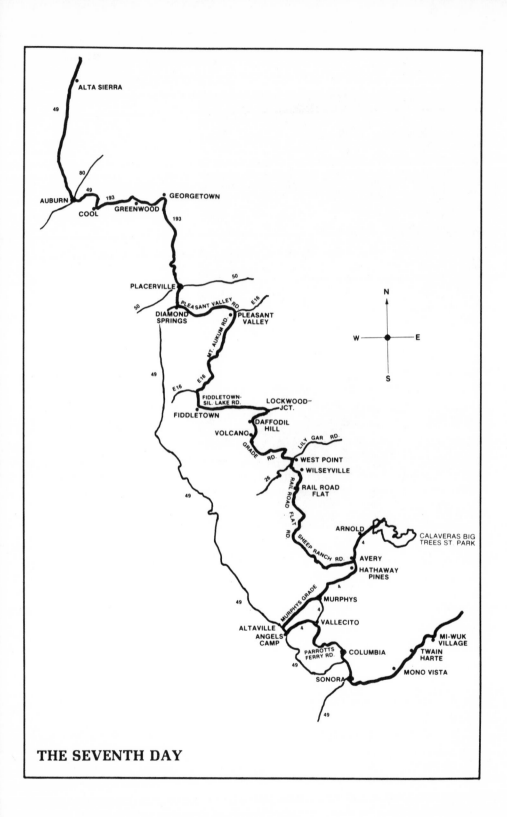

THE SEVENTH DAY

THE **SEVENTH** DAY

On our seventh day of driving we continued to explore the Mother Lode Country, written about so brilliantly by Mark Twain and Bret Harte.

South of Auburn we drove through a tiny village with the intriguing name of Cool and agreed that it is a neat little village well-named.

State 193 follows a loop through farm land sprinkled with a great variety of trees. Just off the road in the village of Greenwood is a marker which reads: "John Greenwood, trapper and guide who came to California in 1844, established here a trading post in 1849. The mining town of Greenwood which developed during the gold-rush days boasted a theatre, hotels, 14 stores, a brewery, and 4 saloons. Among its illustrious citizens was John A. Stone, a California song writer who was buried here in 1863." The monument efficiently serves a dual purpose—atop it is the town fire bell.

In Georgetown, a tremendous building which has weathered the years since '49 is today the IOOF Hall. Georgetown is delightful, with many fascinating old buildings, including a charming hotel. In front of an ancient building occupied by the telephone company rests a big pumping engine from 'way back.

Soon we were traveling through a densely wooded canyon where far below us flowed the South Fork of the American River. Farther south on this river is the spot where gold was first discovered in California. There the river is wide and deep and flows rapidly.

As we entered Placerville, one of the most famous of the early mining towns, we were greeted by many enchanting old buildings which have been faithfully restored. although it has become somewhat "touristy," Placerville is well worth exploring.

At Diamond Springs we enjoyed driving Pleasant Valley Road, an alluring, scenic road through cheerful country.

On Mt. Aukum Road near Pleasant Valley Village, a large field

Historical marker with a dual use, at edge of Greenwood.

*Old mining machinery outside the local office of the telephone
company in Georgetown.*

Curious turkeys near Pleasant Valley Village.

was crowded with thousands of turkeys. As I left the car to get a picture, Betty warned, "Careful. Approach them slowly. They scare easily and may run away."

Surprisingly, they ran toward me.

"Cats and dogs all come to you—now it's turkeys. What's your magic with animals?"

"They sense my kindliness," I replied.

"Yes, I can see it in their little beady eyes."

On to Aukum, River Pines, and Fiddletown, where a giant forty-foot fiddle rests on the roof of the Fiddletown Community Club. A few houses, stores and a tavern are left of this once thriving mining town, now "famous" mostly for its big fiddle.

On our way to Daffodil Hill we stopped to pick wild black raspberries in a fine patch along a shady spot in the road. Poor Bet got

This is the entire village of the once flourishing mining town of Railroad Flats.

Fiddletown Community Club.

caught in the middle of a clump and it wasn't easy to extract her. But the berries were good, probably not too wild as they were sweet and delicious.

Volcano was once a large mining town with several dozen hotels and saloons. Some say in the "old days" it was the largest and roughest town in California. Today, it's an affectionately preserved, small, peaceful village, much of which remains as of old. The stone general store has been in continuous operation since 1852 and looks it, inside and out. Even the film we bought there was "old." There's an extremely fascinating three-story hotel with extraordinary architecture and the surprising name St. George Hotel. The old stone jail and many other curious things are still as they were long ago.

From Volcano we proceeded to Pioneer, West Point, Wilseyville, Rail Road Flat (the town is gone except for an odd-looking general store), Sheep Ranch, Avery, and Arnold. What a fabulous area—the Old West of roaring, golden days—not dead, just sleeping in blissful peace.

Jail of the Gold Rush days at Volcano.

As we drove along, Betty remarked, "There's going to be another great discovery around here."

"You mean more gold?"

"You bet!" she exclaimed. "The developers will soon discover that this whole beautiful and wonderful area is a developer's dream. They'll strike it rich."

"Yes, I'd like to live around here. We could really enjoy life here."

"That's just it," she explained. "Once the developers start dramatizing the glories of the Mother Lode Country there'll be another rush—a rush to bring all the gold back again."

This is typical of the lovely old roads in the Mother Lode country.

Calaveras Big Trees State Park is well named.

In Calaveras Big Trees State Park, which was our next stop, stand tremendous Sequoias, many of which are more than 300 feet high and thirty feet in diameter, and perhaps 3,000 years old. Sequoia trees are protected in state parks, but elsewhere their extermination is threatened by exploitation. The Big Trees State Park is particularly magnificent.

Old miner's shack in Columbia.

After leaving the park we doubled back to Murphys, another of the many fine old villages to which the Mother Lode gave birth. There we took the Murphys Grade Road to Angels Camp, made famous by Mark Twain's "The Celebrated Jumping Frog of Calaveras County," the masterpiece of Western literature that won Mark Twain his first fame.

From Angel's Camp we wended our way to Columbia, perhaps the most captivating of the restored mining towns. Columbia was the climax to our journey through the Mother Lode country, and our time there was enjoyable and rewarding. (Note: State 49 between Placerville and Sonora is popular with tourists, and many of our readers may wish to explore that stretch of 49.) Sonora, like Placerville, is an enchanting old mining town that has stayed very much alive.

We headed west, stopped at Twain Harte, and then drove through Confidence to Mi-Wuk Village for the night. Bret Harte, who became well known for his colorful western stories, encouraged Mark Twain in his writings. During the gold rush days, Harte established the *Overland Monthly*. He wrote such celebrated stories as "The Luck of Roaring Camp" and "The Outcasts of Poker Flat."

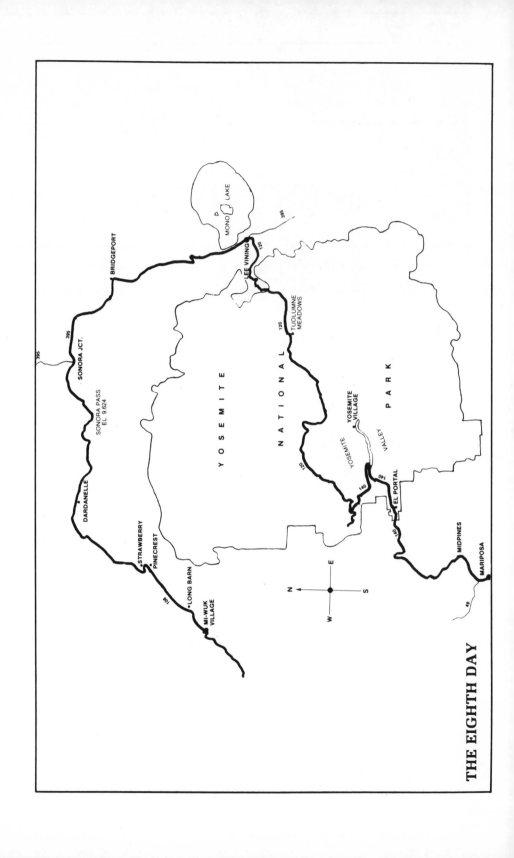

THE EIGHTH DAY

THE **EIGHTH** DAY

We left Mi-Wuk Village for our eighth day of driving, and headed for Sonora Pass, one of the most famous of early mountain
passes. On the way we drove through Pinecrest and Strawberry,
small villages serving as headquarters for an extensive and popular
ski area. Everywhere was wilderness. We knew there must be
activity around us, but there was little evidence. The whole trip to
the Pass is inspiring—stately trees, majestic rugged mountains,
deep canyons, mountain streams, and tremendous boulders. We
felt far away from today's ever-increasing troubles and close to the
simple, quiet, and natural state of being. Again we said, "Isn't it
wonderful to start the day surrounded by the simple beauties of
nature—no fight with freeway traffic."

Betty thought she spotted Dead Man's Creek, which was completely dry. But a minute later she said, "No, that was Eagle Creek
that's dead. Here's Dead Man's Creek with water. It's alive and
healthy."

At Kennedy Meadows we came to an open gate across the road.
In winter there must be many times that this gate is closed to traffic.
From there on, the climb becomes much steeper. A sign advises
house trailers not to go farther. We shifted gears from fourth
down—not to third or second, but into first gear. 7,000 feet, 8,000
feet—we were high, but nearby rocky peaks without vegetation
towered above us.

At 9,624 feet we reached Sonora Pass. Leavitt Peak (at 11,570
feet) was on our south and Sonora Peak (11,462 feet) majestically
pierced the sky to the north. The possibility of a pass here was first
suggested in 1862 by a man named Fletcher.

As we descended into Mono County the scene changed to rolling
meadows with mountains in the distance, more foliage, and land
much less rocky. The road to the meadows was steep and winding.
On the floor of the valley we came to the farming community of

Boulder country near Strawberry.

Sheep grazing peacefully near Bridgeport.

Levitt Meadows. There we saw pastured quite a few riding horses for the many pack trips that originate from this point.

The east side of the mountains is completely different from the west. There are great varieties of deciduous trees. In the fall the colors must be magnificent. There seem to be more sheep than cows. Just before we reached Bridgeport we passed an extensive pasture of perhaps 1,000 or more sheep.

Part of the trip from Bridgeport to Mono Lake reminded us of Switzerland—gently sloping hills with rugged mountains in the distance—masses of colorful wildflowers running up to the snow line.

Mono Lake (6,409 feet) is big and blue with a desolate island in the center. The shores are white and salty. The water is much saltier than ocean water. Nothing seems to live in or around Mono Lake.

Just beyond, at Lee Vining, we entered Yosemite National Park. "Lovely Yosemite," said Betty. "A beautiful day. The sun is just right—you'll get some great photographs."

Mariposa County Courthouse with English-made clock.

I shocked her with my answer. "I'm not taking any."

"No pictures of all those big boulders dumped into the Merced River?"

"Nope."

"Or the cliffs, the pinnacles, the lovely lacy waterfalls, the gigantic trees, the mirror lakes—? Art, do you feel all right?"

I tried to explain. "How many times have you been to Yosemite? Many others have visited this immensely popular park many times. Much has been written about it. Many really fine photographs have been shown in many books. Most of our readers already know a great deal about Yosemite. So this time let's just go slowly and lazily through. This is one of the great wonders of California—let's enjoy it to the fullest."

Betty had a hard time giving up. "Look! Look over there. There's a picture I bet no one else has taken."

We did enjoy Yosemite again, and I without the camera. One never seems to tire of coming back again and again to marvel at old wonders and discover new.

All too soon we left Yosemite and headed for Mariposa, where we discovered the charming Mariposa County Courthouse. Although it was late in the afternoon, we chanced a picture. The sign in front reads, "Mariposa County Court House, California's oldest seat of justice still in use. The front half of the original building completed in 1854 cost $12,000. The lumber was whipsawed from nearby forests. Framework fastened with morticed joints and wooden pegs. Finishing lumber was hand planed and nailed with square cut nails. Fire proof brick vault to protect records added in 1861 was later enlarged. The English-made clock with its 267 lb. bell in the cupola, was installed in 1866 and has been faithfully tolling each hour since. The courtroom, scene of many famous legal battles, civil and criminal, remains the same as in pioneer days, with the original seats, tables, and judge's bench."

On Highway 140 near the north end of town is the museum of the Mariposa County Historical Society, a place well worth the time for a visit. An old restored stamp mill is demonstrated in operation at times during several months of the year, and there are many other excellent displays.

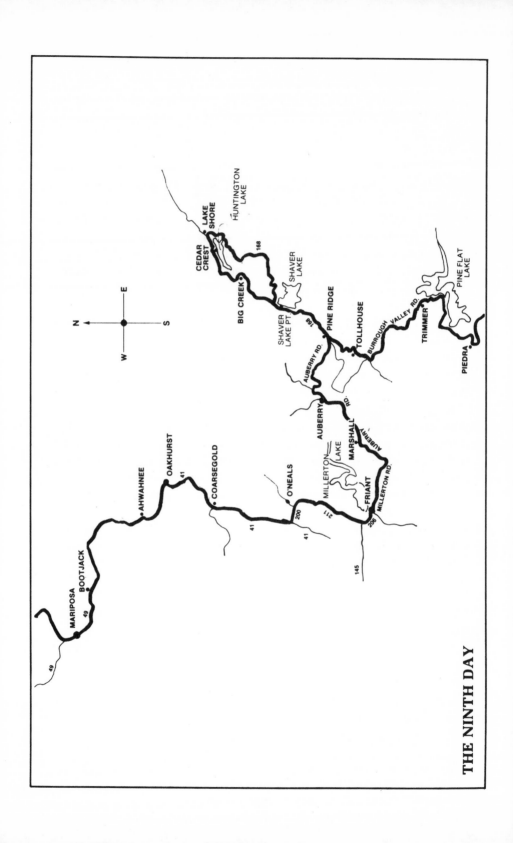

THE NINTH DAY

THE **NINTH** DAY

From Mariposa, still on State 49, we traveled through a pleasant, hilly, farming and grazing area, quite sparsely populated. Just outside of Oakhurst our attention was attracted by an old Conestoga wagon with its original equipment. We examined it with great interest.

From Oakhurst we continued on State 41 toward Coarsegold. Betty wondered what happened to 49—the road seemed to have disappeared. "Isn't 49 the famous road that runs through the Gold Country?" she asked. "Where does it start?"

"It begins up in the Feather River Country..."

"Isn't this Coarsegold? And a few miles over there is Fine Gold and Fine Gold Creek and Little Fine Gold Creek. And there's Quartz Mountain...they find gold in quartz, don't they? There must have been gold around here, but they've ended famous 49. It's not fair to Mother Lode."

We were driving through lovely farming country; near Friant a windmill and old-time water tower seemed to typify the whole area. Cows were grazing everywhere.

"Why are cows sacred in India?" Betty wondered.

"It's their religion."

"Cows here must have a better religion. Look how comfortable they are. Here they peacefully roam the beautiful countryside. In India they mess around in dirty streets and are all skin and bones. Here they are well fed."

"Uh, huh...for the market."

"That's life. Guess long life is the only advantage in being an Indian cow."

Between Friant and Auberry we passed through large patches of sage, their characteristic fragrance filling our car.

Auberry is an attractive small town. Next to the Ponderosa Jus-

Completely equipped old Conestoga wagon, north of Oakhurst.

tice Court an old water tower is so covered with vines that only the roof and door are visible.

We decided to take the loop up to Shaver Lake and Huntington Lake. On the way we had lunch on the shore of inviting Shaver Lake. After lunch we gassed up at Shaver Lake Point, where a sign over the drinking fountain says, "Old Facefull."

Huntington Lake, at an elevation of 6,950 feet, is a brilliant gem set high in the midst of big rocks and deep forest dramatically surrounded, in the distance, by slate cliffs sheared off straight and resembling building-like formations. This is Sierra National Forest, another glorious part of California so difficult to describe adequately yet so easy to enjoy—a favorite hideaway area for Fresno people.

As we reached Pine Ridge we picked up Tollhouse Road to Burrough Valley Road, then on to Trimmer and Piedra. All day we

Proud water tower near Friant.

Curious cows in the Millerton Lake countryside.

Nature has taken over on the main street of Auberry.

Betty was dwarfed by a huge boulder on Shaver Lake.

were in truly back country. There were few cars and only the smallest of villages.

We were enjoying the day so much and time had passed so quickly that we had given no thought as to where to spend the night. I asked Betty where a good place would be. After a long look at the map and the Auto Club accommodations book she said, "Well, let's see, there was nothing at Tollhouse or Trimmer. Nothing here at Piedra. Nothing at Centerville, Squaw Valley, Minkler, Dunlap, Miramonte, Pinehurst, Cedar Brook . . ."

I interrupted. "This should be a good area to build a motel."

"And spoil it?"

"How about staying in Fresno?" I asked kiddingly.

"After a lovely day like this—how could you ruin it with a night in a big city?"

"Maybe a nice farmer would take us in," I further jested.

Betty folded the map. "Just drive on. We'll find something."

We settled on a nice small motel near Fresno.

65

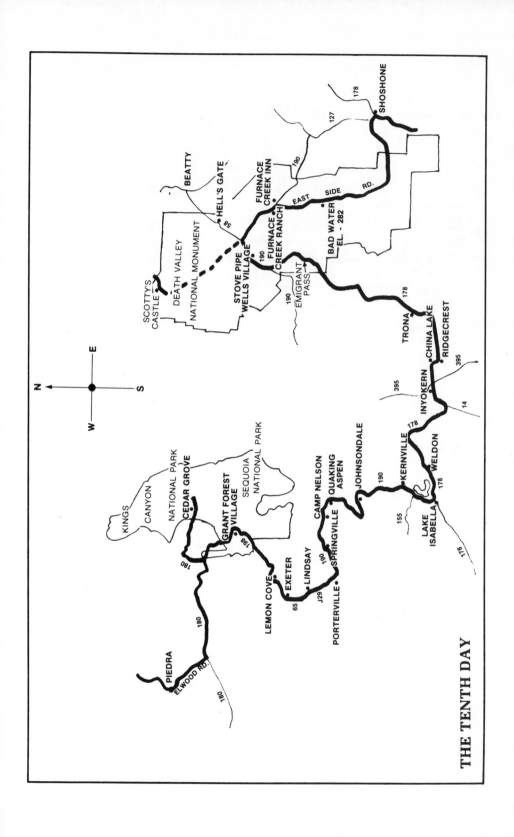

THE TENTH DAY

THE **TENTH** DAY

After changing roads so many times the day before and traveling in such wilderness 'way off "the beaten path," we realized that even out-of-the-way, little-traveled roads are well marked in California. In touring the state searching for country roads to lead us to the unspoiled beauty of California, we have found that it is still around us for all to see, and the roads to it are plainly marked.

At Piedra we crossed the Kings River and followed this spectacular river through Wonder Valley, a very charming valley surrounded by magnificent mountains. There are many large ranches; one is "California's First Dude Ranch."

We reach Kings Canyon Road and proceed to Kings Canyon National Park and Sequoia National Park. At the entrance to the parks the elevation is 6,000 feet. (Kings Canyon and Sequoia are virtually one park.) We were impressed with the gigantic size of the Sequoia trees. General Grant, described as the World's Biggest Tree, measures forty feet in diameter and is said to be 3,500 years old—one of the oldest living things. But General Grant is just one— there are grove after grove of thousands of these tremendous Sequoias, many of which seem comparable in size to General Grant.

In the Parks we discovered majestic granite mountains and deep canyons. Mt. Whitney, the highest point in the continental United States, is there. So also is the Western Divide, separating western flowing waters from eastern flowing waters.

Betty was impressed. "General Grant! Just think, 3,500 years old! Just standing there quietly, serenely, and magnificently all that time. What a happy life."

"What do you mean?" I asked.

"Well, we people tear around struggling to make a living and to find happiness. Then we give up in three score and ten years—while the Old General just stands still in one lovely spot and lets the rest of the world take a beating. He's happy and not about to give up.

General Grant, 3,500 years old and the world's biggest tree.

Three score and ten years are hardly a minute to him. Look up at him—listen to his whispering."

"Maybe he's trying to tell us something," I suggested.

"He's purring!"

Three Rivers is just outside the Parks—and it's like entering another world—a tremendous, wide round valley that looks like a giant basin. Large groves of orange and other citrus trees hug the road. Lemon Cove is a small village crowded in by vast citrus and olive groves.

"I'd like to live here," I fancied.

"You mean in Lemon Cove?"

I continued, "Just think, with all this lovely fruit and luscious olives how easy it would be to make an old-fashioned or a dry martini."

"Calm down. It's not cocktail time yet."

On we drove through rolling hills with grove after grove—dates, almonds, apricots and other fruits—this is one of the great fruit-growing regions of California.

Porterville has a wide, invitingly-landscaped main street. Trees and bushes are planted in attractive groups which project into the street, giving a refreshing effect. Other cities should take note.

At Quaking Aspen we followed the Western Divide Highway through Johnsondale, Roads End, Fairview—a splendid trip along the high ridge (over 6,000 feet) with deep canyons beside us and majestic peaks in the distance.

Soon we were at the bottom of a thickly wooded canyon with a fast-flowing stream (Kern River) which we followed to Kernville. We saw happy fishermen casting in the river—it certainly looks like an excellent place for trout. On the map, between Johnsondale and Lake Isabella, are symbols indicating many camping sites, though none was visible. Apparently this is an outdoorsman's paradise.

Betty lamented, "Poor old Isabella. She looks thirsty."

"Yes, I noticed coming down here quite a few of the lakes were low. Remember the man at the Inn last night said there's been no rain for many months."

Dramatically, Betty implored, "Oh, heavens above, pour down your water of life upon this lovely lady of the lake."

"Who said that?"

"Me."

On our way from Lake Isabella to Inyokern we passed through

THE TENTH DAY

*Nature carved this likeness of George Washington,
twelve miles west of Emigrant Pass.*

an imposing stand of Joshua trees, then climbed over Walker Pass at 5,250 feet. At Freeman Junction we learned about Walker from a monument: "In 1834 explorer Joseph R. Walker passed this junction of Indian trails after discovering nearby Walker Pass. Death Valley '49er parties were diverged west and south after their escape from Death Valley enroute to the California gold fields. Later this became a junction point where the bandit Tiburcio Vasquez preyed on traders travelling between the Kern River mines and Los Angeles and mines of Bodi and the Panamints."

After China Lake and Ridgecrest, fairly large twin towns, we passed Trona, composed mostly of a few houses and a large chemical processing plant, and soon entered Death Valley. Between Trona and State 190 we traveled on Wildrose Road, which the local people call the "Scenic Road to Death Valley."

We followed the floor of a winding canyon with barren mountains so close that in places the sun is unable to find the road—complete shadow and utter barrenness for miles—no evidence of civilization anywhere. Then suddenly we came to a lush little oasis with flourishing trees and bushes. One tall slender tree stands far above the others there, inviting way-worn travelers to be refreshed. The road hairpins around the lonely oasis.

"Imagine the joy of '49ers when they found this spread," I conjectured.

"It's paradise. Let's stay."

"There's no Sambo's."

We continued to climb to what the map calls Emigrant Pass, but a sign at 5,547 feet said Nemo Crest. Twelve miles farther on, still in the barren rocky mountains, we both exclaimed at once, "George Washington!" Sure enough, a stone face about thirty feet high is formed in the mountainside. It certainly resembles Washington from several angles.

"Old George really looked like that," Betty observed.

"You mean that looks like Old George."

"That was here long before Old George . . . What about the Indians?"

I was confused. "Now what've Indians got to do with George Washington?"

"They say the country is 200 years old, and he's the Father of our Country," she explained. "Well, long before Washington that stone face was here, and Indians were all around. They probably had an

71

Lonesome John's blacksmith shop in Death Valley.

old chief who was father of *their* country. It's a shame we spoiled that lovely country."

"Bet if Old George could come back he'd agree with you."

Stove Pipe Wells is another, but much larger, oasis in Death Valley. A marker reads, "Burned Wagon's Point. Here the Jay Hawker group of Death Valley 49er gold seekers from the middle west who entered Death Valley in 1849 seeking a short route to mines of central California burned their wagons, dried the meat of some oxen and with starving animals struggled westward on foot."

Today, Stove Pipe Wells is a popular watering stop and resort that boasts a post office, restaurant, store, gas station, motel, saloon, and many relics of the old days.

A little ways farther we went through the Devil's Corn Field. All around us were what looked like staked stalks of corn but in reality are a unique type of desert brush.

At Sand Dune Junction the road splits, going north to Scotty's Castle and south to Furnace Creek.

Turning south, I said, "We should go back to Scotty's Castle sometime. He was quite a guy and the fabulous castle sure proves what an unusual character he was. It's a unique showplace all right."

"Wonder who Scotty really was?" Betty asked.

"I met him once. His name was Walter Scott. I remember he drove Franklins."

"What are Franklins?"

"That was an air-cooled automobile . . . "

"He wasn't dumb," she interrupted.

"He is supposed to have gained great wealth from a secret gold mine someplace here."

"But there's no gold here."

"Oh, yes, there was some, but legend has it that a wealthy Chicago insurance man named Johnson supplied Scotty with money because he liked Scotty and the fun things he thought up and did."

Betty wondered, "How could he build such an amazing house and live here?"

"He loved the Valley. Its solitude is alive with all kinds of unique plants and small animals—and just look at the beauty around us."

"He's the only man to ever *live* in Death Valley!"

"No, the Panamint Indians once lived here."

(Note: It is recommended that while traveling in the Valley you make the short trip up to see Death Valley Scotty's Castle.)

On the road to Furnace Creek we stopped to read a marker: "Old Harmony Works—on the marsh near this point borax was discovered in 1881 by Aaron Winters who later sold his holding to W. T. Coleman of San Francisco. In 1882 he built the Harmony Borax Works and commissioned the superintendent J. W. S. Perry to design wagons and locate a suitable route to Mojave. The work of gathering the ore (called cotton ball) was done by Chinese workmen. From this point processed borax was transported 165 miles by 20-mule teams to the railroad until 1889." We looked at the old borax plant. There isn't much left now except the old boiler which was used in processing the ore.

Furnace Creek, the largest oasis in Death Valley, is a resort complex composed of Furnace Creek Inn and Furnace Creek Ranch, about half a mile to the north. The Inn is principally a hotel, restaurant, and pool.

THE TENTH DAY

*Desolate old shack seen from Harmony Borax Works
north of Furnace Creek.*

Old Dinah at Furnace Creek Ranch.

The Ranch, really a small village, covers a larger area and offers a golf course, motel cottages, facilities for campers, stores, cafeteria and coffee shop, saloon, museum, and gas station. Headquarters for the Park are also there.

Interestingly, the pool at the Inn is drained daily and refilled with the 80-degree water flowing from the spring. The released water from the pool flows down to the Ranch to irrigate the golf course and landscaping.

At the entrance to the Ranch rests a huge old steam tractor. The marker reads: "Old Dinah 1894—steam tractor and wagons introduced to replace the 20-mule teams and later replaced in turn by the Borate and Daggett Railroad. The tractor was later used and abandoned on the Beatty-Keane Wonder Mine Road in Death Valley."

75

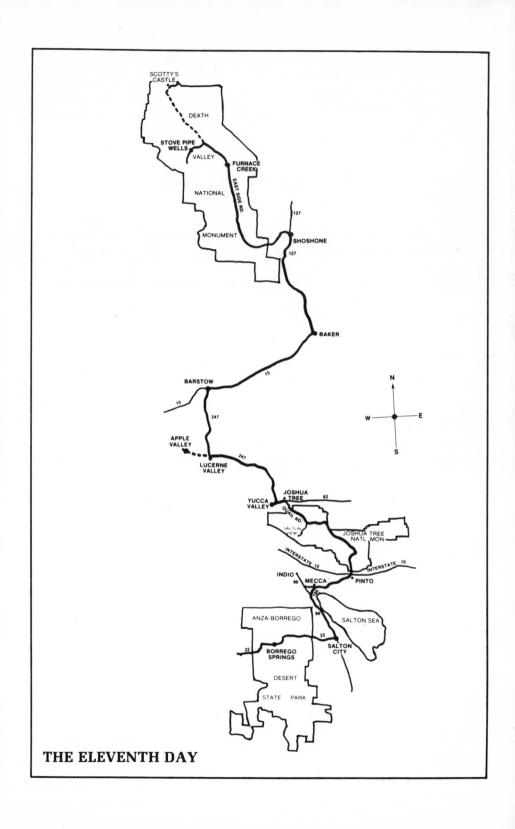

THE ELEVENTH DAY

THE **ELEVENTH** DAY

South of Death Valley most of the road is below sea level. We came to a small, colorful, rocky area called Artist's Palette. A sign there reads: "Various mineral pigments have colored these volcanic deposits. Iron salts produce the red, pinks and yellow. Decomposing mica causes the green. Maganese supplies the purple. Colors of the palette are reproduced on a larger scale on the mountains around Death Valley."

A little farther on is spectacular Golden Canyon. "Recent water run-off has carved this canyon through sedimentary rock which is approximately ten to fifteen million years old," we learned from tourist information.

Badwater is a small shallow pond. As we approached a man was touching the water and then his tongue. I asked him how it tasted. "Pretty salty," he grinned. Badwater, the lowest point in the Western Hemisphere, is 282 feet below sea level. Across the Valley, Telescope Peak has an 11,049-foot elevation, while directly behind us is a shear cliff straight up to Dante View, 5,475 feet. Up the cliff 282 feet is a sign that gave us a queer feeling. It says simply, "Sea Level." As we left Death Valley, Betty said sorrowfully, "I'm sad—I love Death Valley."

"I know—you want to buy a house in Death Valley, but Scotty's is the only home and it's not for sale—thank goodness!"

"No. It's the name."

"Whose name?"

She explained, "Did you notice how beautiful Death Valley is? How clear and sunny? No fog or smog. So many intriguing and fascinating places to see and to explore. How the nights are ... "

I was impatient. "Okay, so Death Valley is a great place. What's all this name business? And why so sad?"

"Well, with a name like Death Valley it's got to be good—and it really is. There's no other place in the whole world like Death

The well-weathered character of Death Valley near Artist's Palette.

Valley, but just because the name is so depressing few people come here. I'm sad about the name."

"That's great! If you changed the name to Paradise Valley, the developers would move in and spoil everything!"

"You're right. Death Valley is alive and well!" she replied happily.

South of Shoshone we came to an area as barren as Death Valley but completely different. Small buttes surrounded us. The fantastic rock formations suggested villages; others looked like connected apartments with Greek architecture.

Some miles farther on we turned toward Barstow.

"What road are we on?" Betty was amazed.

"Interstate 15."

"I thought we weren't going on any freeways."

"That's right, but I took this one on purpose."

"But why?"

"Well, you've enjoyed the roads so far? It was a great chance to relax and see the countryside? We've been seeing things you couldn't possibly see driving on main roads?"

Roy Rogers' Museum at Apple Valley.

Big wheels outside the Apple Valley Museum.

"Sure, sure, but why suddenly go on a freeway?"

"So that you'll appreciate even more when we get back on a back road."

Examining the map, Betty understood. "Oh, I see, you can't get to where we're going without a freeway."

"Sad, isn't it?"

"*. . . everywhere is beauty*" *at Joshua Tree National Monument.*

There was traffic galore speeding in both directions, but we soon reached Barstow and left the freeway, without regret.

At Lucerne Valley we decided to hop over to Apple Valley, a town of about 7,000 people located ten miles to the west of us. The Roy Rogers Museum there is fascinating. This small shack served not only as a sheriff's office but also as a Wells Fargo pickup station, assay office, post office, justice of the peace court, pony express, coroner's office, Indian agent, and many other things. The Museum now contains curious mementoes of the Old West. Outside is an old water trough, a high-wheeled dray, and other reminders of days gone by.

We returned to Lucerne Valley and soon came to a broad, level, flat, uninteresting desert without trees, bushes, or other signs of life, except that in this large desolate area a developer has scattered hundreds of small one-room houses everywhere. A sign says, "a home with 27½ acres." As far as we can see, these little houses dot the desert—a quite unbelievable sight!

Betty remarked, "Who would live there? No TV aerials. Where do they get water? They don't seem to have people either—look how many houses are boarded up."

"There can't be enough hermits in the world to occupy that many little houses." I was also puzzled.

"Surface of the moon" between Salton City and Borrego Springs.

Soon we found that there are much lovelier parts of Lucerne Valley. South of the village of Joshua Tree we entered Joshua Tree National Monument. Tremendous boulders greeted us on all sides. Everywhere is beauty—bewitching Joshua trees—great areas of wild flowers that turn this wilderness into a garden—springs surrounded by stately palms and cottonwood trees—riverbed washes with magnificent rock formations unlike anything else we had ever seen.

Salton Sea, 238 feet below sea level and saltier than the ocean, is slowly becoming even saltier. Fish have adapted themselves to the salt water, but how much longer they can continue to adapt is a question.

The first part of the road to Borrego Springs from Salton Sea was barren but spectacular, with low mountains quite different from any we had seen. About halfway to Borrego Springs the area becomes rocky, extremely dry-looking, wind-roughed rock, without a speck of vegetation.

Betty commented, "You know where we are? We're on the moon!"

"Where's the green cheese?"

"Seriously, all around us it's completely barren—not a smidgen of vegetation. And did you ever see rocks and formations like this? It really does look like the surface of the moon."

"Gives you an eerie feeling."

As we came nearer to Borrego Springs, the character of the desert became less rocky and flatter, with more vegetation. Many ocotillo tower above the low desert plants. In the spring a riot of color brings people from miles away to see the desert in bloom with hundreds of varieties of profusely colored wild flowers. This beautiful part of Anza-Borrego State Park is about eight miles east of the village of Borrego Springs.

We came to a pile of rocks, a monument to Peg Leg Smith. One sign beside the monument reads: "Thomas L. Smith, better known as Peg Leg Smith, 1801 to 1866, was a mountain man, prospector and spinner of tall tales. Legends regarding his lost mine have grown through the years. Countless people have searched the desert looking for its fabulous wealth which possibly could be within a

A reminder of Denmark's "little mermaid" in Borrego Springs.

Big ocotillo on the way to Palm Canyon.

few miles of this monument." Another sign says: "Peg Leg Smith Monument. All those who seek gold add ten rocks to this monument." Desert Steve started the monument years ago and it has grown into a huge pile.

Eight miles down the road we entered the engaging village of Borrego Springs. In the center of town is Christmas Circle, a hub from which five roads radiate into the desert. Borrego Springs, which has become a popular winter resort for desert lovers, is completely surrounded by magnificent Anza-Borrego State Park. Thus contained, Borrego Springs resort activities and growth will ever remain close to Christmas Circle.

We enjoyed exploring the area. A hike to Palm Canyon was especially enjoyable. On the way we found a great variety of desert plants, rock formations and considerable evidence that Indian tribes lived there long ago. At the end of the trail is a lush oasis, closed in by mountains and watered by a gently-flowing stream shaded by stately palms.

Round concretions in Pumpkin Patch east of Borrego Springs.

Because of the varied and inspiring terrain in the Park, many hiking, motoring and jeep trips originate from the Village.

"You know Palm Springs?" Betty asked.

"Of course."

"Well, I bet Palm Springs thirty years ago was like Borrego Springs today."

"You mean this will be another Palm Springs?"

"Why not? Look around you. A lovely desert valley surrounded by beautiful mountains and perfect weather. A nice little village, golf courses, wonderful hiking and exploring—Borrego Springs has everything Palm Springs has except crowds and smog. Wait till those people on the other side of the mountain discover this side."

I answered her, "Don't worry. Borrego Springs is completely surrounded by Anza-Borrego State Park. It can never become a nice big Palm Springs."

"Good! Let's come back soon and stay longer."

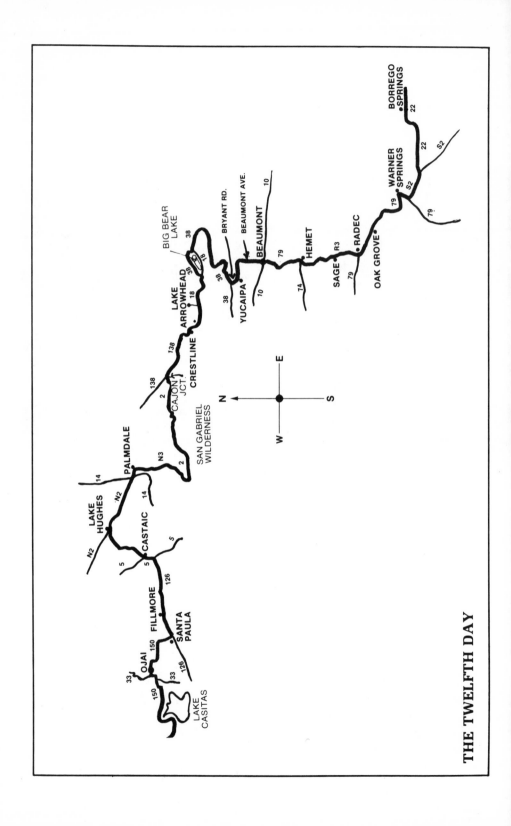

THE TWELFTH DAY

THE **TWELFTH** DAY

Reluctantly we left Borrego Springs and immediately began climbing and winding through almost barren mountains. High up we got a glimpse of Borrego Springs and the surrounding widespread valley—a magnificent view. It reminded us of a Shangri-La. We reached the top and then descended into a completely different country—more trees, more foliage, more rolling pasture land, more farm houses. We were in a valley at an altitude of 3,100 feet as we entered Warner Springs, a pleasant, quiet, leisurely-paced village. We looked around and took a photo of the quaint little Chapel of St. Francis, built in 1830.

The countryside between Warner Springs and Hemet begins with lush foliage, many tremendous live oak, some cottonwood and sycamore, then turns into enjoyable winding roads through low mountains. The ever-changing scenery offers low land, high land, a countryside of farms and ranches, a beautiful region of boulders—thousands of them. As we neared Hemet ahead of us was one of the most exquisite rainbows we have ever encountered.

Betty sang softly, "Oh, what a beautiful day..."

"If only I could get a picture of that. It's the biggest, widest, most beautiful rainbow I've ever seen... so, so close to us..."

"And two pots of gold! You can see both ends."

Hemet, nearby San Jacinto, and Gilman Hot Springs are quiet winter resort towns clustered on a broad level plain at an elevation of 1,200 feet. When we reached Beaumont we decided the fifty-eight miles between there and Borrego Springs is an exciting area well worth further exploring.

Beaumont is spread out insignificantly alongside Highway I-10. Thousands speed by every day. Few bother to get off the highway and visit Beaumont to see whether or not it is well named.

I told Betty, "We just passed over Interstate 10. It stretches from

Chapel of St. Francis at Warner Springs.

Los Angeles to Jacksonville, Florida without a stoplight. Maybe sometime we should write a book on 'Touring Number Ten.'"

She replied, "Yuk! What would you see?"

On Beaumont Avenue we proceeded north toward Big Bear Mountain and Big Bear Lake. The road winds pleasantly through a far-reaching fertile valley with many cherry trees—famed Cherry Valley. It's amazing that so close to Los Angeles and all its suburbs, you still find unspoiled country roads like this one.

Yucaipa seemed to us to be a contented town. It is principally noted for a unique display of animals from around the world. We soon left the valley and started climbing, mountains on both sides. In San Bernadino National Forest the mountains are much closer and steeper. We continued climbing—to 5,000 feet and truly majestic scenery. These are called the Big Bear Mountains, and we certainly felt the bigness—big country—big in beauty—big in every way.

At Camp Angelus we were in ski country. Many chalets and quaint cottages are occupied in winter for skiing and eagerly sought after in summer as places for escape from heat. As we climbed to 6,000 feet we looked down to a small valley with gently sloping hills and a few houses—another Switzerland. We discovered many alluring trails. Clearly, the inviting sweep of those beautiful sloping hills suggests thrilling cross-country skiing and wonderful hiking.

At Onyx Summit (8,443 feet) it was quiet and peaceful. We felt as though we were tiptoeing through nature. The trip through the wilderness from Yucaipa to Big Bear lake is glorious, but we could not catch its breathtaking beauty with a camera. It is too vast—we could only enjoy it "on the spot." State Highway 38 is rightly designated as a scenic highway.

Big Bear City consists mostly of attractive winter and summer houses and Swiss-styled chalets. North Shore Road hugs the lake perhaps forty feet above, so we had an excellent view of Big Bear Lake.

We came to what looked like a white observatory almost in the middle of the lake, with a man-made stone pathway leading to it. Betty wondered what it was. We agreed that it looked like an observatory, but couldn't understand why it was in the middle of a lake. When we reached the path leading out to the building, we learned the answer. A sign there reads: "Big Bear Solar Observatory, California Institute of Technology, operated by Hall

Big Bear Solar Observatory, Big Bear Lake.

Observatory. Purpose of the Observatory is to study the sun. It is located in the lake to reduce image distortions by heat rising from the ground."

Soon we turned off toward Lake Arrowhead. Lake Arrowhead City is really just a small square, rimmed with attractive shops. A clean, Swiss-like community with many chalets, it is quite enchanting. A number of unoccupied docks around the lake suggest plenty of activity in the summer.

We returned to State 138 and after passing the tiny village of Crestline we started downhill to the Valley of Enchantment, which sounded exciting. Many beautiful trees overhang the gently winding road. The region around Silverwood Lake is the popular Silverwood Lake Recreation Area, a state park.

Beyond the turnoff to Interstate 15 the scene began to change. We saw gigantic smooth boulders, mountains of them, with low vegetation peeking out of crevices—a most dramatic sight. They are called Mormon Rocks, and we realized we had never seen anything quite like them. A marker just beyond the rocks reads: "In June 1851, 500 Mormon pioneers came through this area to enter

Yucca south of Palmdale.

the San Bernadino Valley where they colonized and established a prosperous community. Erected by Sons of Mormon Pioneers, May 15, 1937." The monument is a square pile of rocks, quite attractively formed, with an old wagon wheel projecting from the top.

Soon we turned west toward Pearl Blossom onto State 2, another Scenic Highway.

91

Architecture typical of Ojai and Montecito.

On Blue Ridge we were surrounded by great masses of snow-covered mountains far above us. A small sign says that in this part of Los Angeles County there are hundreds of miles of hiking trails used by Boy Scouts and others who like to hike. It is a thrilling and enchanting wilderness.

Ahead, at a little road to the south a sign reads, "Mt. Wilson 5 miles." On this mountain, with an elevation of 5,710 feet, is located Mt. Wilson Observatory, established in 1904 and operated jointly by Carnegie Institution and the California Institute of Technology.

Just beyond we headed north on Angeles Forest Highway through steep mountains. There was some low brush and more yucca than we had seen before in one place. Betty suggested that I should get a picture.

"I got a yucca photo at Borrego Springs."

"But these are yucca in the San Gabriel Mountains."

"One yucca is like every other yucca. No one could tell the difference—except maybe another yucca."

Betty was disgusted. "Did 'yuk' come from yucca?"

We left Palmdale headed toward Lake Hughes. This rolling, green, pastoral country is scattered with ranches and farms. Both mountains and valleys were green with a variety of trees. From Hughes Lake to Castaic we enjoyed lush, rocky canyon country with a gently flowing stream by our side and many varieties of deciduous trees as well as evergreens. Wild flowers were everywhere—a most refreshing area. We noticed a number of picnic spots. This is apparently a "Sunday afternoon drive" for people who live around here.

The dam at Castaic is big and so is the lake it forms. There we met Interstate 5, the West Coast's north-south super-duper highway. Reluctantly we eased onto it, passed Magic Mountain, and quickly and happily got off at State 126.

Relaxing again, Betty exclaimed, "Wow, that was close!"

I was alarmed. "What happened?"

"That three miles on that horrible number five."

"Do you realize that horrible thing runs from Canada to Mexico without a stoplight?"

"Who needs it?"

"I'm afraid millions do."

"Don't count me."

Santa Paula is a sunny citrus town surrounded by hundreds of groves. As we came nearer to Ojai, the countryside slowly changed to more general farming, with many walnut trees.

Ojai is charming, built almost completely in old Spanish architecture. The plaza, Libbey Archways, bell tower, post office, and fire department are especially elegant. A large artist colony and many art galleries indicate the character of the town.

Betty said she would like to live in Ojai. I replied, "Lovely town, but what's the matter with our nice little Carmel Valley?"

"You're in a rut."

"I like my rut."

Betty insisted, "The climate is wonderful here—there are so many..."

I interrupted, "I've heard this record before. You played it in Marin County, Inverness, Sonoma, Graeagle, Downieville, Murphys—I could go on."

"I love California. Too bad we can't afford six California homes."

How could I argue with that?

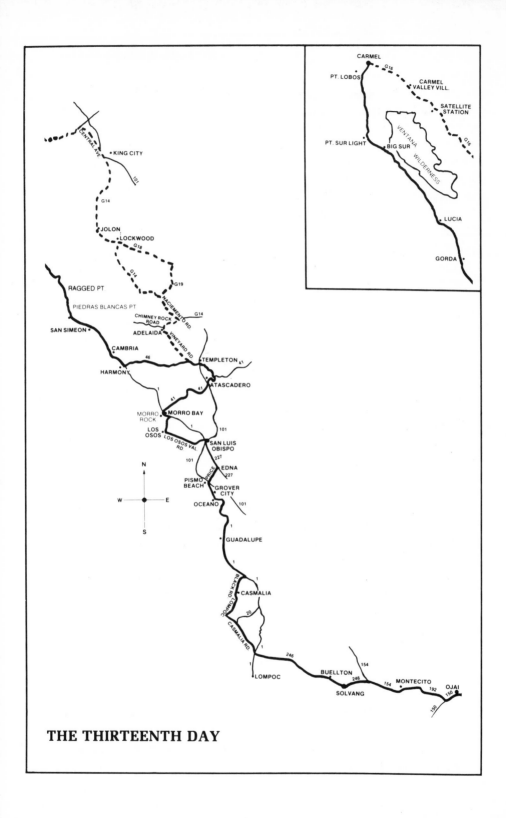

THE THIRTEENTH DAY

THE **THIRTEENTH** DAY

We headed for Solvang on the road back of Santa Barbara. Along this road are many fine estates hidden in the forest. Montecito is a particularly delightful suburb of Santa Barbara.

We drove over the old Marcos Pass and then into Solvang, the picturesque Danish town that is becoming too popular with tourists but still maintains its old Danish architecture and atmosphere. It has many fine motels and quaint little restaurants—a good place for fun and relaxing.

Just beyond is La Purisima Mission State Park. The large mission, established by Father Fermin Lasven on December 8, 1787, was damaged by an earthquake in 1812 and abandoned in 1834. It is now expertly and faithfully restored and is said to be the only example of a complete mission in California.

At Lompoc we joined State 1, the most spectacular of California Scenic Highways, and headed for Quadalupe, Arroyo Grande, Edna and San Luis Obispo. This whole region is cheerful rural country, with rolling hills and large pasture lands in wide valleys sprinkled with wooded areas.

At San Luis Obispo we inspected the old Franciscan mission, San Luis Obispo de Talasa. Built in 1772, it is now a parish church.

Betty declared, "Junipero Serra was a great man. Just think—he built this mission way back in 1772 when we were mad at England and there was nothing out here but wild animals."

"Yes, and in 1776 he built San Francisco de Asis and earlier, in 1770, when old Portola couldn't find the harbor of Monterey, he just casually meandered up to Monterey and built the San Carlos Borromas Mission."

She stopped me, "It's not in Monterey."

"He moved it to Carmel and made it his headquarters and then proceeded to build missions a day's journey apart up and down the California coast."

Gift shop in Solvang.

Betty said, "What I was trying to say is that there were thirteen colonies..."

"What do the colonies have to do with Serra?"

"I'm trying to tell you there was nothing out here then, but back East big things were going on and everybody lived there."

"So?"

At the entrance to La Purisima Mission.

"Well, look what Father Serra started with his chain of motels. Look at California today. Now everybody lives *here*."

We took the Los Osos Valley Road to Morro Bay with its picturesque harbor well protected from the sea by a long finger of land and gigantic Morro Rock. So many visitors return to Morro Bay again and again to enjoy its stirring beauty and exciting activities.

On our way to Atascadero we traveled through rolling hills, then around mountains, and eventually over Devil's Gap. Outside of Atascadero are many farms. One is Belmont Farms, and it surely did remind us of Kentucky.

Cambria is a modern town with many impressive homes of highly imaginative design. It is inspiring to tour casually through the residential section.

At Ragged Point we entered Los Padres National Forest. "Land of many uses," the sign there says. We were on Cabrillo Highway,

The huge rock which guards the entrance to Morro Bay.

named for Juan Cabrillo, who discovered California in 1542 when he landed at Point Loma Head in San Diego Bay. This is the part of California's Scenic Highway Number One that is so renowned.

As we continued toward Big Sur we were close to the ocean, with steep mountains on the east jutting out into the ocean every so often, the road obediently following. With such incredible scenery and majestic beauty, it is easy to understand why Cabrillo Highway is often compared in beauty and character to Amalfi Drive in Italy.

Big Sur is in a small stand of big redwoods—a general store, a post office, a motel and a camping area—surrounded by the Pfeiffer-Big Sur State Park with tremendous Ventana Wilderness just to the east. It is a bewitching area where people come to be near nature—a place where mountains, trees, animals, and rivers are uniquely combined to produce indescribable beauty. Big Sur in-

The "Amalfi Drive" of California, near Big Sur.

spires a feeling of peace and calm that sets you free from today's disturbing world. The feeling stayed with us as we continued north on California's fabulous Highway One. We passed popular and beautiful Point Lobos State Park.

Betty asked, "Not going into Point Lobos?"

"We know every inch of Point Lobos and besides I have hundreds of photographs, and so have thousands of others."

She persisted. "It's such a beautiful park. I thought maybe we could sit in some quiet beauty-spot and..."

"We'll be in Carmel and at the mission in a couple of minutes."

"That's just it. And our lovely trip will be over. I wanted to prolong it."

"It *was* wonderful—and so are you."

99

*The beauties of California will linger on though
a lovely journey comes to an end.*

WEEKEND TOURS

The complete "tour" is a large, irregular oval route which takes you around California on beautiful and interesting country roads. No matter where you live in the state it is not far to *your* starting point.

Many may wish, for time reasons, to enjoy a short tour, or weekend tour. Here are a few suggestions:

San Diego-Los Angeles Area
Refer to maps for Days Eleven and Twelve. You'll find a loop trip between Borrego Springs and Lucerne Valley. Join this round trip from the point nearest you.

Santa Barbara-Monterey Area
Refer to the map for Day Thirteen. Here's another loop between Templeton and Carmel—partly shown with dotted line.

San Francisco Area
Refer to Day Two. Starting at the Golden Gate or Inverness, travel to Petaluma, Sebastopol, Sonoma and the Wine Country to St. Helena on lovely rustic roads for a relaxing weekend.

Northern California
Refer to the map for Day Three. From Redding proceed west and take the Trinity loop around this magnificent lake and wilderness area.

Sacramento Area
Refer to maps for Days Seven and Eight. Here's a golden opportunity to explore the Mother Lode country and/or the area around and through Yosemite.

Fresno-Bakersfield Area
Refer to maps for Days Nine and Ten. Delightful Huntington Lake, Kings Canyon and Death Valley are close to people living in East Central California.

POST-TRIP

On June 7, 1968 the first Scenic Highway in California was designated. The tour outlined in this book frequently follows Scenic Highways and there are others nearby as you go along. You may wish to take "side trips" to explore and enjoy some of these beautiful areas—or plan trips later to include some of them. Following is a list of the Scenic Highways of California:

Route	Miles	Description
1	78.1	Ragged Point to Route 68
1	17.1	From Route 101, near Las Cruces to near Lompoc
1	26.2	Santa Cruz County line (south of Ano Nuevo Pt.) to Half Moon Bay
2	55.3	Angeles Crest Highway from La Canada to San Bernardino Boundary (near Route 138)
4	55.8	East of Arnold to Route 89
5	59.0	From Route 152 to Alameda County line (near Livermore)
9	3.4	Saratoga to Los Gatos
12	11.4	East of Santa Rosa to London Way (near Aqua Caliente)
20	6.5	Between the Skillman Flat campground and one-half mile of Lowell Hill Road
33	23.2	From 6.4 miles to 23.3 miles north of Route 150 and from 30.5 miles to 36.8 miles north of Route 150
35	19.6	Skyline Boulevard from Half Moon Bay Road (Route 92) to Route 9
38	15.6	0.1 mile east of South Fork Campground to 2.9 miles south of Route 18 at State Lane
49	41.2	From the Yuba County line to Yuba Summit
62	8.8	From Route 10 to San Bernardino County line
68	13.9	From Monterey to Salinas River
74	47.7	Between the west boundary of the San Bernardino National Forest and Route 111 in Palm Desert
75	9.0	San Diego-Coronado Bridge Structure and on to Imperial Beach
78	18.2	From the west boundary of the Anza-Borrego Desert State Park to the east boundary
84	45.5	Between the Contra Costa County line and route 160

Route	Miles	Description
88	20.0	From the Amador County line to Route 89 at Picketts Jct. and from Route 89 at Woodfords to the Nevada State line
89	29.8	From Mono County line to El Dorado County line
89	4.4	From 3.2 miles west of Route 395 to the Alpine County line
91	4.2	From Route 55 to east city limits of Anaheim
101	20.5	From 4.5 miles north of Orick to 0.5 mile south of Del Norte County line and from 5.5 miles north of Klamath to 2.5 miles south of Crescent City
125	2.0	From Route 94 to Route I-8
152	15.8	From the Santa Clara County line to I-5
154	32.3	From Route 101 via San Marcos Pass to Route 101
156	4.2	From 1 mile east of Castroville to Route 101
168	16.3	From Bishop to Lake Sabrina
190	55.5	From the west boundary of the Death Valley National Monument to the east boundary
243	27.7	From Route 74 to Banning
385	18.0	From Independence north to Fish Springs Road
395	8.9	Between a point 1.1 miles north of Route 203 and a point 8.9 miles south
580	0.4	From the San Joaquin County line to Route 205
580	10.1	From San Leandro City limits to Route 24

INDEX

Numbers in italics refer to the photographic inserts.